A FLUFFLE BUNNIES

and other fun
collective nouns

Little Lion Publishing UK

Written by Stephanie Lipsey-Liu and

Illustrated by Jemma Dando

For Isabella
and Toby

First printed 2021

ISBN 978-1-7399336-0-9
Little Lion Publishing UK
Nottingham, England
www.facebook.com/littlelionpublishing

This Little Lion book
belongs to

....

What's that? Is it a bunny?
Two bunnies?
No, it's a whole fluffle of bunnies!

Did you know?

Rabbits can jump as high as 3 feet upwards. That's about as tall as a 3-year-old child!

A baby rabbit is called a kit, a female rabbit is called a doe and a male rabbit is called a buck.

There are many other names for a group of rabbits which include a bury, a colony and a flick.

Buzz buzz, eek! A bike of bees!
Don't worry, they won't sting you, they
are too busy looking for nectar.

A group of bees can also be called a:

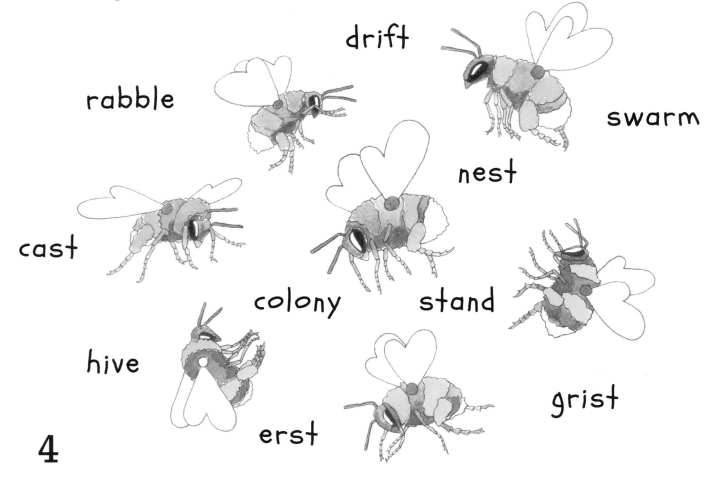

drift

rabble

swarm

nest

cast

colony   stand

hive

grist

erst

Phew! Who knew there were so many ways to describe a group of bees?

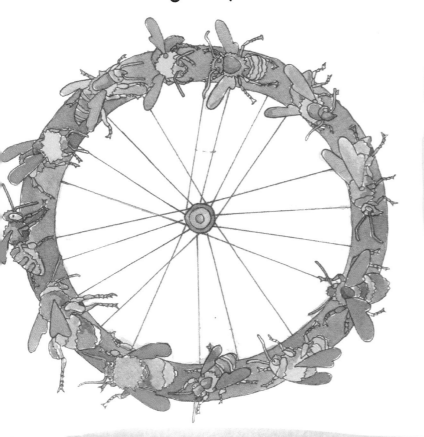

Did you know?

All worker bees are female and it takes one bee her entire life to make ONE teaspoon of honey.

If you find a bee on the ground and she is too tired to fly, get an adult to help you put her onto a flower. If there aren't any flowers, you can give her a little bit of sugar water (not brown sugar).

Who's next? It must be a roll of armadillos!
Armadillos roll their bodies up to protect themselves from predators.

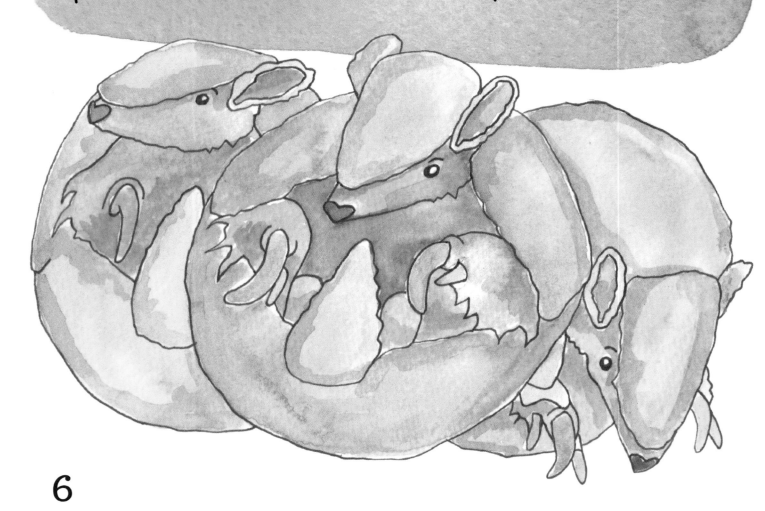

If you ever see more than one armadillo together, you can also say a pack or a herd of armadillos.

Did you know?

Armadillos can't see very well so they have to hunt for their food using their sense of smell.

Can you remember the name for a group of bunnies? Turn to page 2 to see if you were right!

Meow! Gotcha! A pounce of cats.

8

Did you know?

Cats originally developed their meow to communicate with humans, not with other cats.

There are many fabulous terms for a group of cats. You can call them a clutter of cats, a cluster of cats and a glaring of cats too.

Can you remember 3 names for a group of bees?
Turn to page 4 to see if you were right!

Oh, how fabulous! A flamboyance of flamingos.

Did you know?

Flamingos are born grey. Their feathers turn pink because of the natural colouring in the food they eat.

The oldest known flamingo lived until they were 83 years old! In the wild, they wouldn't normally live past 30.

Can you remember the name for a group of armadillos? Turn to page 6 to see if you were right!

Left, right, left, right, left, right, left! Look out, it's an army of frogs! Caterpillars and ants are collectively known as an army too.

Did you know?

Frogs have been around for over 200 million years! That means frogs were hopping around when dinosaurs walked the Earth.

Frogs are amphibians which means they can live on land or in water. They can breathe in oxygen through their lungs when they are on land and through their skin when they're in water.

Can you remember the name for a group of cats? Turn to page 8 to see if you were right!

These hippos look a tad uncomfortable.
More than one hippo is known as a bloat.

Did you know?

Hippos can't actually swim or float. They stand in water to protect their skin from the hot sun. Sometimes when they run in water, it looks like they are swimming!

A group of hippos can also be called a crash or a huddle!

Can you remember the name for a group of flamingos? Turn to page 10 to see if you were right!

Ha ha ha! He he he! A cackle of hyenas.
A cackle is a very loud laugh.
Can you cackle like a hyena?

Did you know?

Hyenas are actually very intelligent. They are smarter than chimps when it comes to solving problems as a group.

A cackle of hyenas can be made up of up to 80 hyenas. They usually do their "cackle" once they have caught their prey to tell their friends to come and share the feast.

Can you remember the name for a group of frogs?
Turn to page 12 to see if you were right!

So many bats, too many to count! When bats are in flight they're known as a cloud of bats. Sometimes we call them a cauldron of bats.

Did you know bats make up a quarter of all mammals? To find food in the dark they let out a high-pitched sound and listen to the echoes that are reflected back. This is called echolocation.

Can you remember the name for a group of hippos? Turn to page 14 to see if you were right!

Ah, the majestic polar bear, how beautiful. We call a group of polar bears an aurora.

Did you know?

Polar bears have such a good sense of smell, they can smell a yummy seal over a mile away!

Polar bears are usually seen by themselves.

A group of polar bears can also be called a celebration of polar bears.

Can you remember the name for a group of hyenas?
Turn to page 16 to see if you were right!

Oh no! Poor panda, what has he done?
An embarrassment of pandas.

Did you know?

Pandas can poo more than 40 times a day!!

Pandas have an extra stump on their front paws that acts like a thumb to help them hold their food.

Can you remember 2 names for a group of bats?
Turn to page 18 to see if you were right!

We can't leave out the unicorns, can we?
Here we have a blessing of unicorns.

Scotland chose the unicorn as their national animal as it was believed to be the only enemy of the lion, England's national animal.

Did you know?

A group of narwhals (the unicorns of the sea) is also known as a blessing.

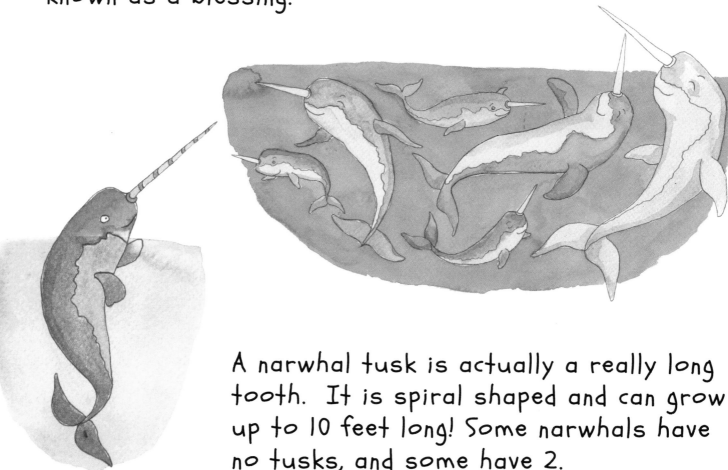

A narwhal tusk is actually a really long tooth. It is spiral shaped and can grow up to 10 feet long! Some narwhals have no tusks, and some have 2.

Can you remember the name for a group of polar bears? Turn to page 20 to see if you were right!

Glossary

Collectively:
As a group. A collective noun is the name for a group of something.

Embarrassed:
Feeling ashamed or shy.

Enemy:
A person who hates or opposes another person and tries to harm them or stop them doing something.

Feet:
A unit of measuring length. There are 12 inches in a foot. One foot is equal to 30.48 cm.

Flamboyant:
Very confident in your behaviour and liking to be noticed by other people.

Majestic:
Having or showing impressive beauty or scale.

Mile:
Unit of measuring length. One mile is equal to 1609 meters.

Nectar:
A sugary fluid made by flowers to attract insects and other animals. It is collected by bees to make into honey.

Pounce:
Spring or swoop suddenly to catch prey. For example, the cat pounced on the mouse.

Predator:
An animal that hunts, kills and eats other animals.

About the Author

Stephanie was born on the Wirral and now lives in Nottingham with her husband, daughter, pack of dogs, school of fish and a Syrian hamster. She is an optician but when she is not testing eyes she can be found sewing, playing the piano, practising sign language, singing and/or adventuring with her family.

About the Illustrator

Jemma was born in Wiltshire in England but now lives in Cardiff in Wales with her fiancée and pounce of cats. When she's not drawing or teaching her lovely little learners, she can be found campervanning, kayaking and climbing mountains.

28

If you enjoyed A Fluffle of Bunnies, look out for our next collective noun book, A Waddle of Penguins.
Coming soon!

A WADDLE OF PENGUINS
and other fun collective nouns

Stephanie Lipsey-Liu   Jemma Dando

We would LOVE it if you could leave us a review on Amazon!
Get your adult to help you with what to write.
If you would like to share a picture of you reading a Fluffle of Bunnies, please tag us on Facebook @littlelionpublishinguk or on Instagram @littlelionpublishing.

29

Draw your favourite animal here!

Can you remember the name for a group of pandas and a group of unicorns? Turn to pages 22 and 24 to see if you were right!

Printed in Great Britain
by Amazon